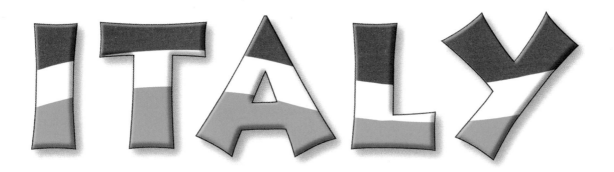

ITALY

Susan Canizares • Betsey Chessen

Scholastic Inc.

New York • Toronto • London • Auckland • Sydney

Acknowledgments

Literacy Specialist: Linda Cornwell

Social Studies Consultant: Barbara Schubert, Ph.D.

Design: Silver Editions

Photo Research: Silver Editions

Endnotes: Jacqueline Smith

Endnote Illustrations: Anthony Carnabucia

Photographs: Cover: Vince Streano/Tony Stone Images; p. 1: Dan McCoy/Rainbow; p. 2: Siobhan Scholter/Picture Perfect; p. 3: Hideo Kurihara/Tony Stone Images; p. 4: Robert Frerck/Tony Stone Images; p. 5: SuperStock; p. 6: Vince Streano/Tony Stone Images; p. 7: Nawrocki/Picture Perfect; p. 8: John Lawrence/Tony Stone Images; p. 9: Harvey Lloyd/ The Stock Market; p. 10: Index Stock; p. 11: C. Seghers/Photo Researchers, Inc.; p. 12: Ian Shaw/Tony Stone Images.

Library of Congress Cataloging-in-Publication Data
Canizares, Susan 1960-
Italy/Susan Canizares, Betsey Chessen.
p.cm. -- (Social studies emergent readers)
Summary: Simple text and photographs explore the sights of Italy, including bridges, statues, gondolas, and fountains.
ISBN 0-439-04572-X (pbk.: alk. paper)
1. Italy--Description and travel--Juvenile literature.
[1. Italy--Description and travel.] I. Chessen, Betsey, 1970-.
II. Title. III. Series.
DG430.2.C35 1999
914.504'929--dc21
98-53369
CIP AC

13 14 15 16 17 18 19 20   08   6 7 8 9 / 0

In Italy, you can see . . .

bridges

and buildings.

You can see steps

and statues.

You can see grapes

and gondolas.

You can see fountains

and food.

You can see castles

and the Colosseum.

Italy.

ITALY

Italy is a peninsula sticking out into the Mediterranean Sea. On a map it looks like a long boot poised to kick the Italian island of Sicily.

Bridges *Ponte Vecchio* means "old bridge." It was built in Florence in the Middle Ages, around 1350, and has houses and shops on it. In the sixteenth century a Florentine prince ordered a corridor to be built on top of the shops on the bridge. This corridor connected his offices, called the Uffizi, to a palace across the river so that the prince could travel safely and secretly between the two.

Buildings One of the strangest buildings in the world can be found in the city of Pisa. It started out as a beautiful but perfectly normal bell tower. But before three stories were finished, it had already sunk into the soft ground on one side. The Leaning Tower of Pisa now leans 17 feet. The tower is closed to people, and engineers are trying to stop it from falling over.

Steps The Spanish Steps in Rome were built to connect the church on top of the hill with Piazza di Spagna below. The steps are an amazing sight: There are terraces, curves, and straight sections covered with colorful flowers.

Statues These statues in Hadrian's villa are almost 2,000 years old. The emperor Hadrian created a villa with buildings that reminded him of his favorite sites in the Roman Empire. The canal in the picture represents the Nile River in Egypt and is surrounded by buildings and statues copied from an Eygptian town.

Grapes These people are following the old tradition of harvesting grapes by hand. Agriculture is very important in Italy today. Most farms are family owned and operated. Tuscany is a particularly sunny and fertile region in northern Italy. Its olive trees and vineyards cover the hillsides, and much of Italy's olive oil and wine are produced there.

Gondolas Venice was built on 120 islands. Venice's main "streets" are its 177 canals. For centuries people used gondolas—flat-bottomed, narrow boats with a single oar—to get around. Today gondolas are used mostly by tourists. In the seventeenth century a law was passed requiring all gondolas to be painted black to prevent competition between noblemen who wanted to have the most splendid gondola. To this day all gondolas are painted black.

Fountains The more than 300 decorative fountains in Rome have been celebrated in art, poetry, and music for centuries. The most famous is the Fountain of Trevi, which shows Neptune, the ancient mythological god of the sea, and other mythical sea creatures. The fountain took 30 years to build and takes up one whole side of a building. A legend says that if you throw a coin into the fountain, you will return to Rome someday.

Food Italians take great pride in their food. In most of Italy, pasta is the most important food. There are over 100 different pasta shapes! Spaghetti is the most well known; some others are conchiglie (shells), farfalle (butterflies), paglia e fieno (straw and hay; this is very fine pasta that looks like straw), and vermicelli (little worms; it tastes much better than it sounds!).

Castles This fourteenth-century castle overlooks the sea on the island of Sicily, the largest island in the Mediterranean Sea. Sicily was invaded many times in its history, and strong castles like these were built on steep hillsides all over the island to deter attackers and warn Sicilians of their arrival.

The Colosseum The Colosseum opened nearly 2,000 years ago and, though partly in ruins today, is still a very impressive building. In this large amphitheater, Romans watched spectacles such as gladiator and wild animal fights. About 50,000 people could be seated in the Colosseum in Rome.

Flag The Italian flag is called the tricolore (tri = three; colore = colors) because it has three vertical stripes of green, white, and red. Some say green was used because it was the favorite color of Napoleon, the ruler of Italy in 1798 when the flag was first used.